THE BIBLE AND
ARCHAEOLOGY

THE BIBLE AND ARCHAEOLOGY

Third Edition, Fully Revised

by J. A. THOMPSON

WILLIAM B. EERDMANS PUBLISHING COMPANY
GRAND RAPIDS, MICHIGAN

To Marion,
my Parents,
and my
past and present Students

THE BIBLE AND ARCHAEOLOGY
© Copyright 1962, 1972, 1982, by Wm. B. Eerdmans Publishing Co.
Printed in the United States of America

Library of Congress Cataloging-in-Publication Data

Thompson, J. A. (John Arthur), 1913-
The Bible and archaeology.

Bibliography: p. 447
Includes indexes.
1. Bible — Antiquities.   2. Bible — History of
contemporary events.   I. Title.
BS621.T52   1982   220.9'3   81-5439

ISBN 0-8028-3545-7   AACR2

Reprinted, November 1988

Printing History:
Substantial portions of this book have appeared before under the following titles and copyrights:
Archaeology and the Old Testament, Copyright 1957, 1959 by Wm. B. Eerdmans Publishing Co.;
Archaeology and the Pre-Christian Centuries, © Wm. B. Eerdmans Publishing Co., 1958, 1959;
Archaeology and the New Testament, © Wm. B. Eerdmans Publishing Co., 1960.
Combined edition first published 1962; fourth printing 1969. Revised edition 1972. Third edition, fully revised 1982.

FOREWORD

The three shorter studies which have been brought together in this volume were first published in a series called Pathway Books. As I was one of the consulting editors of that series, I have a prior interest in introducing this work; but that is not my principal reason for doing so. My principal reason is that I believe this work, now revised, brought up to date, and so lavishly illustrated, to be a very useful handbook for Bible readers.

Dr. Thompson has for long made a special study of biblical archaeology. For a number of years he was Director of the Australian Institute of Archaeology in Melbourne. He has had practical experience in archaeological field-work with the American Schools of Oriental Research at the sites of Roman Jericho and Dibon. And as lecturer in Old Testament Studies in a theological school he knows how to relate the findings of archaeology to the wider interests of biblical study.

Archaeology certainly makes an important contribution to the study of the Bible. Large areas, especially of the Old Testament, have been so greatly illuminated by it that it is not easy to imagine what readers made of them before the days of biblical archaeology. Yet the scale of its contribution can be exaggerated, and it is one of the merits of Dr. Thompson's book that it does not make exaggerated claims for archaeology or try to make it fill a role for which it is unsuited. For all the light that archaeology throws upon the text, language, and narrative of the Bible, it is improper, and in any case unnecessary, to appeal to it to "prove" the Bible. Archaeology has indeed corroborated the substantial historicity of the biblical record from the patriarchal period to the apostolic age, but it is not by archaeology that the essential message of the Bible can be verified.

Sometimes, indeed, archaeology has made the interpretation of the biblical narrative more difficult rather than less so. It has happened at times that an earlier phase of research has appeared to solve one particular problem satisfactorily, whereas later study has thrown the whole question into the melting-pot again. This has happened, for example, with Professor Garstang's interpretation of the Joshua story in the light of his Jericho excavations, and with Sir William Ramsay's solution of the Quirinius problem in St. Luke's Gospel.

There is no finality in biblical archaeology. As more pieces of the jigsaw puzzle come to light, we see that we have sometimes put previously discovered pieces into the wrong place and produced a distorted pattern. Archaeological surveys for the Bible student must therefore be subjected to repeated revision in the light of new knowledge. Such a revision now lies before us, and it is to be hoped that Dr. Thompson's survey will have many readers, and will guide them to a better understanding of the Bible story.

University of Manchester   —F. F. BRUCE

PREFACE

The present volume contains the material which formerly appeared in the three smaller Pathway Books *Archaeology and the Old Testament* (1957, 2nd ed. 1959), *Archaeology and the Pre-Christian Centuries* (1958, 2nd ed. 1959), and *Archaeology and the New Testament* (1960). These smaller volumes have now been brought together into one volume with some rearrangement, and with the addition of more recent information, new maps, and numerous relevant and excellent photographs. Reference to more recent works is made in footnotes, and additional quotations from the ancient records of the Near East have been woven into the text.

The aim of the volume is to provide a concise resumé of the information that is now available for the study of the biblical records as a result of many years of excavation in Bible lands. In so short a compass there can be no pretense of being exhaustive. Indeed many important items have been mentioned only in passing, and significant books in French and German with their wealth of detail have been given very scant mention. Many have not even been cited. This results from the fact that this volume is intended in the first place for English-speaking readers who are not familiar with other languages. In a few cases the footnotes will point to some of these works. But the Bibliography at the end of this volume will provide a list of larger works in many of which the diligent reader will find comprehensive reading lists.

Regrettably, only passing reference can be made at present to the contributions of the Ebla archives. Despite the immense potential of the tablets for biblical studies, as yet they have been examined only cursorily, and much of the scholarly interpretation remains embroiled in controversy.

It is some gratification to the author to discover that the material of the three Pathway Books, which originally comprised lectures given in theological college, Bible college, and university classes in Australia in the past decade, should prove of value to similar classes in America.

Special acknowledgment should again be made of the help given by the author's wife in the preparation of this composite volume and of the encouragement of the Publishers.

The author's hope is that this larger volume will continue to prove useful to students who are learning their first lessons in Biblical Archaeology.

—J.A.T.

TABLE OF CONTENTS

INTRODUCTION

PART ONE:

ARCHAEOLOGY AND THE OLD TESTAMENT STORY
UP TO 587 B.C.

PART THREE:

ARCHAEOLOGY AND THE NEW TESTAMENT

LIST OF MAPS

LIST OF CHARTS

LIST OF ABBREVIATIONS

AASOR: *Annual of the American Schools of Oriental Research*
AJA: *American Journal of Archaeology*
ANET: *Ancient Near Eastern Texts*
BA: *Biblical Archaeologist*
BAR: *Biblical Archaeology Review*
BASOR: *Bulletin of the American Schools of Oriental Research*
BJRL: *Bulletin of the John Rylands Library*
EAEHL: *Encyclopedia of Archaeological Excavations in the Holy Land*
ICC: *International Critical Commentary*
IDB: *Interpreter's Dictionary of the Bible*
IEJ: *Israel Exploration Journal*
JAOS: *Journal of the American Oriental Society*
JBL: *Journal of Biblical Literature*
JNES: *Journal of Near Eastern Studies*
JTS: *Journal of Theological Studies*
NBD: *New Bible Dictionary*
PEQ: *Palestine Exploration Quarterly*
QDAP: *Quarterly of the Department of Antiquities of Palestine*
RB: *Revue Biblique*
VT: *Vetus Testamentum*

LIST OF ILLUSTRATIONS

xvii

INTRODUCTION

1

BIBLICAL ARCHAEOLOGY TODAY

IN the past forty years a new subject has entered the curriculum of Bible colleges and theological colleges. It is Biblical Archaeology. Its importance is beyond dispute. It is a vital branch of general biblical research, which has made tremendous progress in recent years. One outstanding worker in the field of biblical archaeology and general biblical research has recently written:

> There are few fields of human knowledge where the progress of discovery makes constant revision of handbooks and other aids to study more necessary than in biblical research.[1]

Biblical archaeology has all the fascination of the science of archaeology, which seeks to unravel the story of past ages by digging up their material remains. But it has the added interest that through this study we are better able to understand and interpret the textbook of our faith. Not the least fascinating part of these modern studies is that they go far toward authenticating the history of the written records which are the basis of our faith. Of course, it is impossible to authenticate archaeologically all that is in the Bible. Many of its statements lie beyond the sphere of archaeological investigation. No excavator can comment, in terms of his science, on the simple statement: "Abraham believed God, and it was counted unto him for righteousness." But in its own sphere this science does much for the student of the sacred record.

1. G. E. Wright and F. V. Filson, *Westminster Historical Atlas* (London, 1953), opening article by W. F. Albright, p. 9.

The late Professor Nelson Glueck, one of the foremost biblical archaeologists of the twentieth century, standing near Wadi Ein Irka in the Negeb. (Israel Office of Information)

THE VALUE OF BIBLICAL ARCHAEOLOGY

When we extract from the field of general archaeology all the material that is relevant to the Bible, and then organize our material into a formal study, we have the substance of a course in Biblical Archaeology. Such material has significance for the Bible student in at least four ways.

In the first place, it provides the general background of the history of the Bible. It is not sufficient merely to read the Bible if we wish to appreciate the significance of its narratives. The men of Bible history lived in an environment. Abraham, for example, moved in a world that had its own peculiar customs. It is necessary for us to learn from nonbiblical information what this world of his was like if we would understand more clearly the significance of the things he said and did. We realize that the picture we get of Abraham in the Bible has much about it that is reminiscent of the ancient Middle East in the period of about 1800–1500 B.C. The same kind of thing could be said of Joseph, Moses, Joshua, David, and the whole family of Bible personalities.

Secondly, the Bible is by no means a complete record. It would take a whole library to recount all the events necessary to give a complete account of the experiences of God's people. But there is now a vast amount of nonbiblical material available to supplement our Bible story. The authors of the Bible selected only certain aspects of the life of a man. They did not aim to give us a complete picture. They simply wrote about what was important for their purpose and passed over other things in silence. The archaeologist helps us to fill out the picture. We learn, for example, that King Omri, dismissed in six verses in the book of Kings, was known to the Assyrians and was the conqueror of Moab. We discover that King Ahab sent a large contingent of troops to a great battle against the Assyrians. Neither of these facts is mentioned in the Bible. These and many other items of information are made available to us by the archaeologist. In the following pages we shall discover many of them.

Then, thirdly, biblical archaeology helps us in the translation and explanation of many passages in the Bible that are hard to understand. Sometimes we find a word in a kindred language that gives an alternative meaning which will suit the Bible context better. Sometimes we learn that the Bible has preserved valuable geographical information which we have missed because we did not understand. At other times we gain a completely new impression of a passage in the light of fuller historical knowledge.

Finally, it is perfectly true to say that biblical archaeology has done a great deal to correct the impression that was abroad at the close of the last century and in the early part of this century, that biblical history was of doubtful trustworthiness in many places. If one impression stands out more clearly than any other today, it is that on all hands the overall historicity of the Old Testament tradition is admitted. In this connection the words of W. F. Albright may be quoted: "There can be no doubt that archaeology has confirmed the substantial historicity of Old Testament tradition."[2]

Even if some writers want to speak of divergences from the historical picture, they do so with caution and admit that there is no serious modification of that picture.

THE SOURCES OF INFORMATION

The archaeologist obtains his information from material objects left behind by the people of those far-off days. They are to be found in the ruined towns, graves, and inscriptions of the people. The objects now investigated by the excavator may be either quite exposed to human view even today, or covered up completely or partially by earth.

There are numerous structures that are still quite exposed. We need only refer to the pyramids and temples of Egypt, the Parthenon and other structures on the Acropolis in Athens, the great ziggurat at Ur of the Chaldees, various Roman temples, aqueducts, roads, and the like, scattered all over the East as well as in Europe, and the massive Crusader castles still to be seen in many lands. These buildings are more or less completely exposed and their inscriptions, art work, and general architectural features are readily available to the archaeologist.

Some buildings are partly covered and need to be cleaned up. Perhaps debris has gathered about their lower portions. This has to be cleared away before the complete structure is visible. Some of the buildings already referred to required a certain amount of clearing before they could be made to tell their story.

The completely covered remains, however, are the ones that require the skill of the trained excavator. How did they become covered? By a variety of means. Perhaps the buildings lay in the lower part of a town in early times. Once the town was deserted, the rains brought silt down from the hills around, which, in the course of centuries, covered the town. The marketplace at Athens and the forum at Rome were covered in this way.

Perhaps a town was overwhelmed by such means as volcanic ash. This was the fate of Pompeii and Herculaneum, near to modern Naples, in A.D. 79. Today the archaeologist can clear away the ash and view a Roman town of the first century A.D.

Some of the covered remains are in tombs and graves. These are very important because when people in the ancient world buried their dead, they placed in the grave objects that they believed would be needed by their departed friends in the afterlife. It is from graves that we obtain many of our fine museum

2. W. F. Albright, *Archaeology and the Religion of Israel* (Baltimore, 1955), p. 176.

Bethshan (Tell el-Husn), a town near Mount Gilboa in Israel, has been occupied almost continually since Chalcolithic times (ca. 5000–3200 B.C.). This view is from the Roman theatre. (W. S. LaSor)

pieces. There was no reason for them to be broken since they were protected by the walls of the tomb.

The most important type of covered ruin is that in which we find the remains of several towns one on top of the other. To us moderns this is strange. But in the ancient world, when a walled town was burned, or beaten down by battering rams, or destroyed by an earthquake, the newcomers who rebuilt the town did not remove the debris and the foundations of the old city. They selected the best material for re-use, leveled off the remains, and rebuilt on top of them. Some feet of debris from the previous town would thus be sealed off. The general pattern of houses and streets would remain, and a great many small items would be left in the rubbish.[3]

Most of the towns in Palestine known to us in the Bible are of this type— Bethel, Jericho, Samaria, Jerusalem, Megiddo, Bethshan, Bethshemesh, Debir, Gezer, and so on. Some of these towns had ten or twelve or even twenty strata of destroyed towns. Each recounts its own story. When the whole is excavated by cutting large trenches across the mound and comparing the finds, the story of the town slowly emerges. These sites are known to the archaeologist as "tells" or "mounds."

3. P. W. Lapp, *The Tale of the Tell* (Pittsburgh, 1975).

These, then, are the sources from which the excavator reconstructs his story. The items that speak are the ruined buildings with their walls and rooms and floors, the pottery, the metal implements and tools, the weapons, the ivory work, the glass, coins, and jewelry, the inscribed and written material, whether it be on stone, bone, or baked clay. Indeed, any item at all contributes to the final picture.

Among the most significant of the finds in an excavation are the written records, letters, receipts, census lists, contracts, and literary pieces, written on stone, broken pottery, leather, or papyrus. Material like this has been found in caves, wrapped around mummies, lying about in ruined buildings, or cast out on a rubbish heap. Such perishable material as leather and papyrus requires a dry climate, so that it is normally found only in Egypt above the level of the Nile floods, or in the dry parts of Palestine. Inscriptions in stone are likely to be found anywhere. Often inscriptions were filled with lead, but sometimes they were little more than scratches on the rock (*graffiti*). Occasionally written information was painted on the wall of a tomb, or marked in carbon on a coffin or a wall. Although this written material lacks popular appeal, it is possibly the most important of all the information that can be recovered from an ancient civilization, for it records the names of people and places and gives detailed information of events, laws, and customs.

Coins fall into a special class, for they are of value not only in dating remains, but also because they contain in themselves valuable historical material. They were important instruments of the propaganda machine in the ancient

Babylonian clay tablets (ca. 3100 B.C.) inscribed with linear characters that are directly derived from pictographs. The tablets contain accounts of fields, crops, and commodities. (British Museum)

world, and a study of them gives us a good deal of information about the appearance of kings and emperors, as well as about events. There are several references to coins in the New Testament, for example, the one where Jesus was questioned about the payment of taxes and He asked to see a coin. This was the occasion for an important lesson in loyalty: "Render therefore unto Caesar the things which are Caesar's; and unto God the things that are God's" (Matt. 22:21).

Finally, after several seasons of work, the story is told. The biblical ar-chaeologist hastens to discover whether there are important items in the report of the excavator that bear on Bible history, and that will be of use in one of the ways we have suggested above.

BIBLICAL ARCHAEOLOGY AND THE NEW TESTAMENT

The average Bible reader sometimes gains the impression that the spectacular discoveries of the archaeologist apply only to the Old Testament. This is a serious misunderstanding. The New Testament, too, has benefited greatly from archaeological discovery.[4] To the credit of the modern excavator, there lies an impressive array of material that has not only thrown light on the history of the New Testament period but that has also had important repercussions in the field of New Testament study generally. It is not too much to claim that important modifications have been brought about in scholarly theories about the New Testament, almost entirely as a result of archaeological discovery. We shall notice some of these in this volume.

There is probably a good reason for the development of the idea that archaeology has little to say about the New Testament. The really significant discoveries that bear upon it are not nearly so striking as those that refer to the Old Testament. Many people who know very little about Bible history would nevertheless have heard of Sir Leonard Woolley and his excavations at Ur, the home of Abraham, or of Professor Garstang and his work at Jericho. Again, the excavations of Professor Koldewey at Babylon, the capital of the famous Nebuchadnezzar, seem to be commonplace in history books. The achievements of the great Assyrians have been known for over a century now since Sir Henry Layard, H. Rassam, and George Smith carried out their remarkable researches in the ruins of Nineveh and Nimrud. But all of these are of interest chiefly to the Old Testament scholar. Even the casual visitor to Egypt, Palestine, Syria, Leba-non, Iraq, and other countries in the East sees before his eyes massive structures like the pyramids of Egypt, the great ziggurat of Ur, the widespread ruins of Babylon, the Assyrian palaces of Nineveh, Khorsabad, and Nimrud, and the palaces of the Persians, all of which are of specific interest to the Old Testament

---

4. A. Parrot, *Discovering Buried Worlds* (London, 1955); E. M. Blaiklock, *Out of the Earth* (Grand Rapids, 1957); J. Finegan, *The Archaeology of the New Testament* (Princeton, 1969).

reader. Moreover, all of these are so old and carry with them so much of the mystery connected with those long-past days that, in comparison, Roman remains seem to come from yesterday and to lack the fascination of the more ancient past. Without this glamor, the antiquities of New Testament times have made less appeal to the public and so the impression has grown that there is little of value to be found in the excavation of remains of New Testament times.

Despite the absence of popular appeal, archaeological finds relating to the New Testament are by no means lacking. The most important of them are written records, inscriptions, and papyri. But there are some building remains and a considerable variety of other items which have their own special interest.

For many of the towns mentioned in the New Testament there are still considerable remains above the ground. For others there is a great deal that has become covered through the ages and needs to be excavated. The important town of Jerusalem, which we shall discuss in detail later, is rich in archaeological material.[5] However, when these towns are laid bare by the archaeologist there is much to be discovered, both about the life that was lived in these towns and about some of the buildings that are mentioned in the New Testament. We need only call to mind the great temple of Diana at Ephesus, or the marketplace at Athens. There are other towns unearthed by the archaeologist which, though not mentioned in the Bible, nevertheless tell us much about the life of the times. Such a town is Pompeii, which was overwhelmed by Mount Vesuvius in A.D. 79. Here we have a typical town of Paul's day, and a study of its remains will give us a clear idea of the sort of town in which Paul delivered his message.

5. For details see ch. 19.

PART ONE:

ARCHAEOLOGY AND THE OLD TESTAMENT STORY UP TO 587 B.C.

The remains of the ziggurat (temple tower) at Ur as seen from the southwest. It was built by Ur-Nammu and dates from the end of the third millennium B.C. The structure at Babel (Gen. 11) has been likened to such a tower. (University Museum, University of Pennsylvania)

2

ABRAHAM THE MIGRANT

IT would appear that the writer of the book of Genesis was concerned merely to lay down some general statements about mankind in his first ten chapters and to move as quickly as possible to the story of Abraham. Those general statements concern the creating hand of God behind all things material and living, the universality of human rebellion and of divine judgment, the fact of God's desire to save men, and the fact that men may be saved by faith in God and in obedience to Him.

The author of Genesis took from the information available to him certain data to illustrate his general principles. Unfortunately his sketches are so summary and so carefully selected that it is difficult to provide archaeological support for them. But some useful material is available for comparison along at least three lines.

(a) Creation. There are other ancient stories of creation, the best known being *Enuma Elish*, a Babylonian-Sumerian epic which tells of the origin of the gods from the primeval chaos in which two strange entities, Apsu and Tiamat, were commingled in a single body. From these came the gods. One of the younger gods, Marduk, finally overthrew Tiamat, cut her in two, and formed heaven and earth from her body. He then created man, as well as the rest of the universe. In comparison with this strange story recorded today on seven clay tablets, the majestic narrative of Genesis 1 and 2 stands out as a masterpiece. The one true God created all things in a series of divine utterances.[1]

1. J. B. Pritchard, *ANET* (Princeton, 1955), pp. 60ff., translation of E. A. Speiser; A. Heidel, *The Babylonian Genesis* (Chicago, 1942).

Two of the seven tablets in the Assyrian series containing the Creation epic. They are copies of the older Babylonian text and were made for the Assyrian royal library at Nineveh. The text may be traced to third-millennium Sumerian originals. (British Museum)

At one stage many Old Testament scholars suggested that the biblical story of creation owed much to *Enuma Elish* and made much of the supposed relationship between the Hebrew word *tehom,* "the deep," and the name *Ti'amat,* the goddess who personified the salt sea waters. In fact both *tehom* and *ti'amat* derive from a common Semitic root *thm* which in Ugaritic in the fourteen/thirteenth centuries B.C., and even in Ebla in the twenty-third century B.C., denoted very generally "the deep" or "the ocean abyss." The Babylonian *Enuma Elish* is itself not the original story but is derived from an earlier source. Today we have a number of Babylonian fragments which show a great deal of variation on details.[2]

(b) The Flood. The Babylonian tablets also have a flood story.[3] The hero Utnapishtim was saved in a ship with people and animals from a great flood. There are interesting parallels with the biblical story—the sending forth of birds to discover dry land, the building of an altar, and the offering of a sacrifice. But again, whereas the biblical story of the flood is monotheistic, the Babylonian

2. See A. Heidel, *The Babylonian Genesis* (2nd ed. 1951). Cf. J. V. Kinnier-Wilson in D. W. Thomas (ed.), *Documents from Old Testament Times* (New York, 1958), p. 14, who refers to "no connections of any kind"; W. G. Lambert, "A New Look at the Babylonian Background of Genesis," *JTS,* Vol. XVI, Part 2 (Oct., 1965), pp. 287–300, esp. pp. 289, 291, 293–299; A. R. Millard, "A New Babylonian 'Genesis' Story," *Tyndale Bulletin,* No. 18 (1967), pp. 3–4, 16–18.

3. J. B. Pritchard, *ANET,* pp. 42ff., translation of S. N. Kramer; A. Heidel, *The Gilgamesh Epic and Old Testament Parallels* (Chicago, 1946); A. Parrot, *The Flood and Noah's Ark* (London, 1955).

story is set in a strange polytheistic framework. There are, in fact, many differences between the two stories despite the resemblances, and it is more likely that both stories reach back to an original event than that the Hebrew story is a modification of the ancient myth.

Some features of the Babylonian Flood story have been illuminated by archaeology. The hero of the story, Utnapishtim, was, in fact, one of the early kings of the South Babylonian city of Uruk during the Early Dynastic II period.[4] According to the Babylonian story, this king went in search of immortality.

The story was widespread in the ancient Near East and excavations have yielded quite a number of texts or fragments which refer to the story of the Flood, although these differ in detail.[5] It is mentioned in the Sumerian King List, which gives a list of kings after the Flood and comes from about 2000 B.C.[6] From the seventeenth century B.C. at the latest comes the Epic of Atra-hasis. This originally included the fullest Babylonian account of the Flood.[7] There is a Sumerian Flood story from about 1600 B.C.[8] A Babylonian tablet about the Flood and referring to Atra-hasis was found in Ugarit and dated to 1400–1200 B.C.[9] Most of the Babylonian Epic itself is attested by copies from the early second millennium B.C., but the key Tablet XI is attested only in seventh-century B.C. copies. Ancient Mesopotamia has provided, up to the present, several Flood stories. Of special interest to Bible readers is a Gilgamesh fragment from the middle of the second millennium B.C., that is, from the Middle Bronze Age, found in Level VIII at Megiddo.[10]

Important Akkadian texts come from the library of the Assyrian king Ashurbanipal at Nineveh, although the Gilgamesh Epic is known from versions which antedate the first millennium B.C. A fragment of an Akkadian recension was found in the Hittite Archives at Boghazkoy, as were Hurrian and Hittite translations, both from the middle of the second millennium. Fragments of Tablets I–III and X come from ancient Babylonia and date to the first half of the second millenium.

That there were great floods in Mesopotamia which might have given rise to the Flood story is shown by considerable deposits of silt in several excavated sites such as Ur, Shuruppak, Erech, and Kish where strata of clay were laid down by large floods. The claim by Sir Leonard Woolley that he had found a deposit which marked the biblical Flood is no longer accepted.[11] The deposit there is a thick one but rather localized in one area of the city. The flood deposits in other

---

4. W. C. Hallo, *The Ancient Near East* (New Haven, 1971), p. 46.

5. J. B. Pritchard, *The Ancient Near East, Supplementary Texts and Pictures relating to the Old Testament* (Princeton, 1969), pp. 503–507.

6. W. G. Lambert and A. R. Millard, *Atra-hasis* (Oxford, 1969), pp. 16, 25.

7. *Ibid.*

8. *Ibid.*, pp. 138f.

9. *Ibid.*, pp. 131–133.

10. A. Goetze and S. Levy, "Fragment of the Gilgamesh Epic from Megiddo," *'Atiqot*, Vol. II (1959), pp. 121–128.

11. Sir Leonard Woolley, *Ur of the Chaldees* (London, 1938), pp. 21–23.

sites vary in thickness and in age. None can really be identified as a deposit laid down specifically by the biblical Flood. All we can say is that ancient Mesopotamian literature speaks consistently about a flood. The Flood deposits would seem to support the general truth of this picture. But the date and extent of the biblical Flood are at present beyond our knowledge.[12]

Attempts have been made to locate the remains of the Ark on modern Mount Ararat. Such attempts are virtually pointless since the Bible refers to the mountains (plural) of Ararat (Gen. 8:4) as the resting place of the Ark so that no specific mountain is identified. Further, the very name Ararat refers to the ancient land of Urartu, which covered a wide area. Pieces of timber found on modern Mount Ararat seemed to offer some hope of identification, but when these were dated by modern radiocarbon tests they were shown to be no older than the seventh–eighth centuries A.D.[13]

(c) King lists and their longevity in primaeval proto-history. One of the features of the Mesopotamian king lists is the very considerable age of the kings. The Sumerian King List commences with the words:

> When kingship was lowered from heaven kingship was (first) in Eridu. (In) Eridu A-lulim (became) king and ruled 28,800 years. Alal-gar ruled 36,000 years. Two kings (thus) ruled it for 64,800 years.[14]

The line of kings continues down into historical times which are well known, and the length of the reigns becomes shorter. The significance of these lengthy periods is hardly to be understood literally and must have had some symbolic meaning. They were probably not intended to serve a narrowly chronological purpose in the modern sense. It is of some interest that the Bible also ascribes considerable length to the age of some of the descendants of Noah (Gen. 11:10–32). There is thus a certain parallelism between the biblical and the Sumerian material. But in the present state of our knowledge the significance of this is not clear. The biblical figures are much more modest than their Sumerian parallels.[15]

(d) The literary structure of early Genesis (1–9). Some interest attaches to the literary structure of the early chapters of Genesis, which follow the sequence of creation (chs. 1–2), man's alienation from God (chs. 3–4), a link by a ten-generation genealogy (ch. 5) to the Flood and the subsequent renewal (chs. 6–9), the development of mankind (chs. 10–11:9), and another nine-generation genealogical link from Shem to Terah the father of Abraham (chs. 11:10–25). This scheme is broadly parallel to that of the Sumerian King List, Atra-hasis, and the Sumerian Flood story.[16] It would seem clear that there was a

12. J. Finegan, *Archaeological History of the Ancient Middle East* (1979), pp. 23–26.
13. L. R. Bailey, "Wood from 'Mount Ararat': Noah's Ark," *BA*, Vol. 40, No. 4 (Dec., 1977), pp. 137–146; F. Navarra, *Noah's Ark, I Touched It* (translated from French, 1974).
14. J. B. Pritchard, *ANET*, pp. 265f.
15. See K. A. Kitchen, *Ancient Orient and Old Testament* (Downers Grove, 1966), pp. 35–41.
16. See K. A. Kitchen, *The Bible in its World* (Exeter, 1977), pp. 31f.

common literary tradition in the ancient Middle East differing in details from place to place but maintaining a certain similarity in literary outline. This tradition would seem to have arisen in Mesopotamia and was taken to the West to be given biblical expression at a later date.

The full implications of archaeological work in Mesopotamia have not yet been realized. As year follows year, excavations continue to provide exciting information about that ancient world against which the earliest stories of the Bible have to be set if they are to be understood properly.

After his introductory chapters, the author of Genesis moves into the story of Abraham, for which he provides a great deal more information.

THE ORIGINAL HOME OF ABRAHAM

The Bible places the home of Abraham at Ur of the Chaldees and suggests two stages of his migration to Palestine, first from Ur to Haran and then from Haran to Canaan. The identification of Ur has not been without some disagreement among scholars, some of whom see in the phrase "Ur of the Chaldees" a later editorial note since it seems inappropriate in the second millennium B.C. when the Chaldeans had not emerged into the light of recorded history. There may be some truth in this, but biblical tradition places Abraham's original home at Ur in Lower Mesopotamia (Gen. 11:31). Attempts to locate Ur in Upper Mesopotamia have not been at all successful.[17] Certainly many scholars feel that there are good reasons to give credence to the view that ancient Ur, the modern Tell el-Muqayyar, is the city referred to in Genesis.[18] Such a view is not necessarily tied to a proposal that Abraham was an Amorite and that his migration should be seen as part of the Amorite movements in the early part of the second millennium B.C. But if this identification of the biblical Ur is correct, then the forefather of Israel had contact with high civilization although he may not have actually been a city dweller. The excavations of Sir Leonard Woolley during the years 1922 to 1934 showed something of the splendor of the centuries before Abraham.[19] The royal tombs of Ur, dating to about 2500 B.C., produced a collection of magnificent golden vessels which are still the delight and wonderment of the students of the ancient world. Ur was a town with a complex system of government and a well-developed system of commerce, one with writing in common use for the issue of receipts, the making of contracts, and many other purposes. There were town drains, streets, two-story houses, a great temple tower (ziggurat), trade routes joining the town with other great towns to the north and the south, and various other evidences of a highly developed civilization.

17. See W. F. Saggs, "Ur of the Chaldees. A Problem of Identification," *Iraq*, Vol. XXII (1960), pp. 200–209.
18. D. J. Wiseman, "Ur of the Chaldees," *NBD* (1962), pp. 1304f.
19. L. Woolley, *op. cit.*

Statue (ca. 2500 B.C.) from the "Great Death Pit" at Ur of a he-goat with forelegs in a tree. Probably it was a holder for burning incense or for an offering bowl. The tree and the goat's legs and face are made of gold, the horns, eyes, and upper fleece are lapis lazuli, and the lower fleece is white shell pieces. The belly was made of silver, and the core of the statue was wood. (British Museum)

This area of southern Mesopotamia had formerly been occupied mainly by the Sumerians, who were the first settlers on the plains of Shinar. At an early date Semitic people began to infiltrate into these areas. These became known as the Akkadians. They lived peacefully among the Sumerians and took over their culture. Eventually they became the dominant group and replaced the Sumerians as the rulers of these lands. In later centuries yet other Semites came to dwell here, such as the Amorites and the Aramaeans. There is good evidence that the area was occupied by Semites at an early date. It is not at all unlikely, therefore, that a Semite like Abraham should come from southern Mesopotamia, although we may not be able to tell the precise Semitic group from which he came.

PEOPLES IN THE EAST
IN THE DAYS OF ABRAHAM

It is important to realize that the world in which Abraham lived was a very busy world indeed. We may say that the centuries following 2000 B.C. were centuries of great change all over the East. In addition to the older Sumerians and the Semitic Akkadians who were scattered throughout Mesopotamia, we find other important groups of people, such as the Amorites, the Hurrians, and the Hittities, coming into prominence in these lands.

We hear of the *Amorites* in the Bible among the inhabitants of Palestine and particularly of Transjordan. They were to be found, however, in many lands in the Near East at this time. Just before 2000 B.C. they began to move into Lower Mesopotamia, and by 1800 B.C. they were in possession of most of this region. At the same time they were active in the general area northeast of Galilee, as we learn from a valuable collection of execration (cursing) texts from Egypt. There were two groups of these texts that comprised curses written on small figurines or vessels and directed against potential rebel vassals of the Egyptians. The breaking of the objects on which the curses were written was believed to release curses. The first group of texts written on vases dates to the period between 1925 and 1875 B.C. and lists about thirty Palestinian and Syrian chiefs but hardly a town.[20] A second group of texts written on baked clay figurines and dating to the second half of the nineteenth century B.C., that is, a little later, refers to many more towns and fewer chieftains.[21] The two sets of texts give a picture of Amorites settling down in areas from Galilee northward and eastward. From this area they must have moved south into Transjordan and southwest into Palestine proper. At the time of the Exodus the Israelites overthrew Sihon and Og, kings of the Amorites in Transjordan (Num. 21:21–35), and fought with the Amorites in Palestine (Josh. 10).

An interesting document from Egypt tells the story of Sinuhe, an Egyptian official who fled to the same general area in the twentieth century B.C. He lived with an Amorite chieftain of the same kind as Abraham, Laban, or Jacob.[22]

It was the Amorites who gave to the world the great lawgiver Hammurabi, who ruled during the years 1792–1750 B.C. A study of his code of laws shows a number of interesting parallels with the law code of Moses.[23] This is not really surprising since the Israelite patriarchs came from these lands, and Abraham must have known and lived under similar laws before the days of Hammurabi.

---

20. First published in 1926 by K. Sethe in Berlin and known as the Berlin Texts.
21. G. Poesner, *Princes et Pays d'Asie et de Nubie* (Brussels, 1940).
22. J. B. Pritchard, *ANET*, pp. 18ff.
23. Compare Laws 250–252 with Exodus 21:28–36.

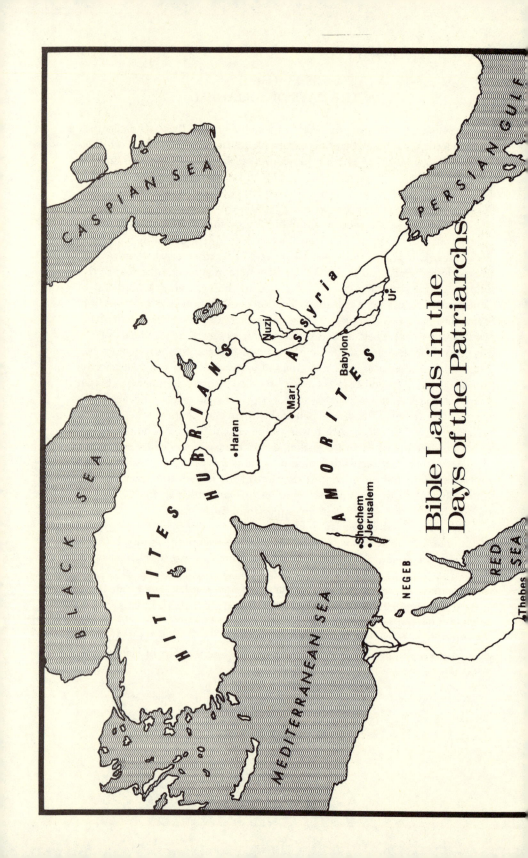

Bible Lands in the
Days of the Patriarchs

CASPIAN SEA

PERSIAN GULF

BLACK SEA

HITTITES

HURRIANS

Assyria

Nuzi

•Haran

•Mari

Babylon•

Ur

A M O R I T E S

•Shechem
•Jerusalem

NEGEB

MEDITERRANEAN SEA

RED SEA

•Thebes

Two typical portraits of King Hammurabi of Babylon (1792–1750 B.C.) surrounded by the well-known Code of Laws. The portrait to the left is cut in limestone (British Museum). The eighty-inch diorite stele to the right depicts Hammurabi receiving the symbols of authority—the rod and the ring—from the god Shamash, seated. (Consulate General, Republic of Iraq)

An important question which has not yet been satisfactorily answered is whether the patriarchs were part of the Amorite movement. Both the forebears of later Israel and the Amorites, and for that matter the Aramaeans and other peoples in western Asia, were part of the general West Semitic stock. Biblical tradition links the patriarchs with the Aramaeans (Gen. 11:32ff.; 24; 29; 30; 31). But there is a good deal of uncertainty still about the ethnic origins of the patriarchs.[24] It is safe to assert, however, that the Amorites were a very significant element in the population of western Asia in the first half of the second

24. For well-documented but very critical assessment of the evidence see J. van Seters, *Abraham in History and Tradition* (New Haven, 1975), pp. 20–26, 33f., 43f., etc.; T. L. Thompson, *The Historicity of the Patriarchal Narratives* (New York, 1974), pp. 55–57, 67–88, 89–93, 118–143, 144–171. Both books have been the object of some very critical comment by other scholars.

millennium B.C. and were part of the scene in which the patriarchs lived and moved.

The second group of people that call for brief mention are the *Hurrians*. They began to enter the lands around the Tigris about 2000 B.C. Some clay tablets of this period introduce a new type of name, different from the other names of the area. These new names are now known to have belonged to the Hurrians, who during the next couple of centuries spread across central Mesopotamia and formed the main population in a number of very important kingdoms like the Mitanni kingdom which occupied the area between the Tigris and Euphrates rivers about 1500 B.C. In recent years the important town of Nuzi to the east of the Tigris has yielded an amazing collection of clay documents which have given insight into the customs of these lands.

Some of these customs bear some resemblance to some of the patriarchal customs portrayed in Genesis. The question will be taken up later in this chapter. But many of the customs which were current among the Hurrians had parallels in Middle Eastern society over many centuries. The Hurrians were only one section of a very complex society, and it is not inconceivable that some of Israel's forebears had contact with the Hurrians somewhere or other.

It may be asked whether Hurrians as such are known in the Bible. Some scholars feel that the Horites correspond to the Hurrians.[25]

The *Hittites* were a third group which became active about the time when the Israelite patriarchs were moving about in the East. This was a group of peoples which originated somewhere in Europe and formed part of the great Indo-European migration that reached as far as India. This group, which is of some interest to the Bible student, settled in Asia Minor. Here they found a more ancient people known as the Hatti people. The newcomers took over their name. References to Hittites in the Bible may not be to the Hittites of Asia Minor. According to the genealogical table of Genesis 10:15, a certain Heth was a son of Canaan. Interpreted in ethnic terms, there was a tribal element in Canaan which might be called the Hittites. Abraham purchased a field in which to bury Sarah from a certain Ephron the Hittite (Gen. 23:10), but he had to do business with the elders of Machpelah who are called "the sons of Heth" (Gen. 23:3, 5, 7, 10, 16, 18, 20). Nothing in this chapter requires that the term Hittite mean any more than a local Canaanite group. Indeed, the Hittites of Genesis are not to be connected with the ancient Hatti people nor to the Indo-European community that came into Asia Minor and gained control over the Anatolian plateau about 1900 B.C. Already in patriarchal times, however, they were active on the fringes of the patriarchal world. In the years *ca.* 1700–1190 B.C. they were to form an empire centered on Hattusa, and after their fall

    25. There is wide discussion on the issue. See R. de Vaux, "Les Hurrites de l'histoire et les Horites de la Bible," *RB*, Vol. 74 (1967), pp. 481–503; *Histoire ancienne d'Israel* (Paris, 1971), pp. 69–71, 86–91; J. van Seters, *The Hyksos* (London, 1966), pp. 181–190; D. J. Wiseman (ed.) in *Peoples of Old Testament Times* (Oxford, 1973); H. A. Hoffner, "The Hittites and the Hurrians," pp. 221–226.

some Hittite centers lingered on in North Syria alongside the Aramaeans. There is no evidence of direct Hittite penetration into Palestine, although cultural influences no doubt were brought in by traders.[26]

Some reference should also be made to the Aramaeans who figure prominently in the patriarchal story (Gen. 25:20; 28:1–7; 31:20, 24; Deut. 26:5). This group of people is not greatly known on written documents in the early part of the second millennium B.C. although the name Aram, as a place name, is known in an inscription of Naram-Sin of Akkad as early as the twenty-third century B.C. Then there are references in documents from Drehem, a city of the Lower Tigris, to a region on the Upper Euphrates *ca.* 2000 B.C. There is also reference to a personal name in the Mari texts (seventeenth century B.C.) and at Alalakh (seventh century B.C.) and Ugarit (fourteenth century B.C.). From Egypt we have a reference to a place name in Syria from the days of Amenophis III (first half of the fourteenth century B.C.), as we do in the journal of an Egyptian frontier official in the days of Pharaoh Merneptah about 1220 B.C. From then on the name occurs frequently in Assyrian documents. It seems clear that a group, later to be known clearly as the Aramaeans from the land of Aram, were already known in the Upper Euphrates area from quite early in the second millennium. It is among these people that biblical tradition looks for the patriarchs and, however ill-defined they are at present, we must count them as one of the groups of people that were present in patriarchal areas in the first part of the second millennium B.C.[27]

To these peoples we must add numerous smaller groups, many of them subtribal in size and belonging to larger ethnic groupings. In Palestine itself from an early age there was already a very mixed population which had received, and was receiving all the time, infusions of migrants from various directions. The patriarchs, then, did not move in a vacuum but in a world that was peopled by a wide variety of ethnic and tribal elements, a picture that is reflected in the patriarchal narratives. Unfortunately we are unable to argue from the presence of these peoples in the biblical narratives anything about the date of the patriarchs since peoples mentioned there were known and were active in the Middle East for many centuries. On the basis merely of the peoples mentioned one could argue for a date for the patriarchs anywhere in the second millennium B.C. or even, with some modification in the meaning of the terms, into the first millennium B.C. Despite this, it is certainly a possibility that the patriarchs fit into the first half of the second millennium.

ABRAHAM'S JOURNEYINGS

The Bible describes the journeys of Abraham in some detail. Leaving Ur, he first traveled north to the town of Haran where he lived for a number of years before

26. H. A. Hoffner, *op. cit.*, pp. 197–221.
27. A. Malamat, "The Aramaeans," in D. J. Wiseman (ed.), *Peoples of Old Testament Times*, pp. 134–155.

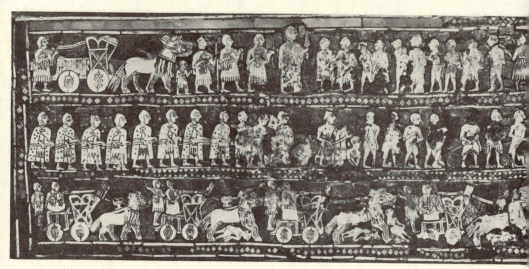

A masterpiece of early Sumerian art, this mosaic standard from Ur (ca. 2500 B.C.) is made of lapis lazuli, shell, and red limestone set in bitumen on wood. The top row depicts a chariot, soldiers, the prince (the large figure), and naked prisoners; the middle row, soldiers and naked prisoners; the bottom row, chariots being driven over a corpse-strewn battle field. (British Museum)

Thirty-seven Semites ("Asiatics") bring eye paint to Khnemhotep III (ca. 1900 B.C.) in a painting in his tomb at Beni Hasan, Egypt. This detail shows a boy with a spear, four women in multicolored garments (which contrast with the Egyptians' plain white robes), a donkey carrying bellows (perhaps for metal working?), and a man playing a lyre. (Oriental Institute, University of Chicago)

setting out again to journey to Palestine (Gen. 12). A later writer in the Bible described this first journey of Abraham as one in which "he went out, not knowing whither he went" (Heb. 11:8b). Recent research suggests quite strongly that this verse must not be applied in a physical sense. There were well-trodden trade routes throughout these lands, and we have no reason to think that Abraham left the usual roads when he made his journey. We should rather interpret this verse in a spiritual sense, namely, that having set out at the call of God, he did not quite know where this response was likely to lead him in the end.

Not only were there great roads from Ur to Haran, but other roads connected northern Mesopotamia with the Mediterranean coast and with Palestine. Still others connected Palestine with Egypt. There was a good deal of traffic between these latter two lands. This is shown by the numerous Egyptian items found in the tombs of Palestine dating to the years 2000–1500 B.C. This period covers the time of the great Twelfth Dynasty (*ca.* 1991–1786 B.C.), the second Intermediate Period, and the Hyksos Period (*ca.* 1720–1550 B.C.) during large parts of which Egypt exercised some sort of control over Palestine. Thus the Execration Texts, already referred to,[28] come from the Twelfth Dynasty, as does a valuable set of paintings from tombs found at Beni Hasan, 250 miles down the Nile, in which the artist has portrayed for us a group of semi-nomads who visited Egypt about 1900 B.C.[29] There were thirty-seven of these people, who were led by a man with a perfectly good Semitic name, Absha. The dress and the equipment of these people give us a good idea of the dress and equipment of the patriarchal family which moved into Egypt about the same time.

During the next two hundred years there was considerable movement to and fro between Egypt and Palestine. More generally there was movement for trade in many areas of the Middle East. One of the most notable examples is the movement of traders from Anatolia to ancient Assyria. From a center in Anatolia at Kanesh (Kultepe) caravans moved to Asshur and back again on a regular basis. Important documents found at Kanesh, the Cappadocian Documents[30] dating to *ca.* 1900 B.C., give valuable information about trade, caravans, legal procedures, and the like, and throw a flood of light on the customs of the period.

It is interesting to discover that the towns visited by Abraham according to the biblical records lie today in the zone where the rainfall is between ten and twenty inches annually. This is a zone where sheep can live. We have no serious reason to think that the general rainfall pattern has changed through the centuries.

---

28. See p. 19.
29. Photo in *Westminster Historical Atlas* (London, 1953), p. 23. See photo, p. 24.
30. O. R. Gurney, *The Hittites* (London, 1964), p. 18.

A drawing of what the ziggurat built by Ur-Nammu at Ur may have looked like. The temple buildings in the angles of the stairs are not shown. (University Museum, University of Pennsylvania)

PATRIARCHAL TOWNS, NAMES, AND BEASTS OF BURDEN

It may be asked whether we have any contemporary evidence about towns mentioned in the biblical records. There is, of course, good evidence for Ur. Some excavation has been undertaken at Haran in recent years, although only in the upper, later levels of the mound. It was known in the important Cappadocian texts of 1900 B.C. The name was still referred to in important texts from Mari on the middle Euphrates coming from about 1700 B.C. The site has never been lost. The name Nahor, as a town, is also attested in these northern areas in the Cappadocian texts, the Mari texts, and late Assyrian texts. It belonged to the district of Haran. Many other towns in this area are known from documents, and sometimes the same name is used for a person in the biblical record. The names Serug and Terah are cases in point.[31]

It is precisely in these northern Mesopotamian lands where the biblical

31. A discussion of place names, as well as of the whole range of modern knowledge now available, has been undertaken by R. de Vaux, "Les patriarches Hébreux et les découvertes modernes," *RB*, Vols. LIII (1946), LV (1948), LVI (1949). See also H. H. Rowley, "Recent Discoveries and the Patriarchal Age," *BJRL* (1949), pp. 3–38; R. de Vaux, *Histoire ancienne d'Israel* (Paris, 1971), pp. 189f.

records place the home of the patriarchs that we find these names. We may conjecture that a good deal of contact took place between Palestine and these lands to insure a continuity of culture. For this reason we look to northern Mesopotamia for the cultural background of the patriarchs.

We now have archaeological information about a number of the patriarchal towns in the Palestine area, such as Bethel (Gen. 12:8; 28:19; 35:1, 15, etc.), Shechem (Gen. 12:6; 33:18; 34:2, etc.), Jerusalem (Salem, Gen. 14:18), Mamre (Gen. 13:18; 14:13, 24; 18:1, etc.), Gerar (Gen. 20:1; 26:6, 17, 20), Beer-sheba (Gen. 21:14, 33; 22:19; 26:33, etc.), and Dothan (Gen. 37:17).[32] Continuous occupation began at Bethel in the Early Bronze IV Age (*ca.* 2200–2000 B.C.), but there was earlier settlement in the area. Bethel was still in existence in Byzantine times. There were settlements in the Beer-sheba area during the Chalcolithic period (*ca.* 3500 B.C.). The modern Tell Sheba dates only to the Iron II Age (*ca.* 1000–586 B.C.), so that no comment can be made about a site at Beer-sheba in the second millennium although the site of Ramat el-Khalil, two miles north of Hebron, was occupied early in the Middle Bronze II period, about 1800 B.C. This site may have been Mamre. The biblical story does not necessarily demand an actual town, however. The case is different with Shechem, which was a town of some sort early in the Middle Bronze Age (about 1850–1750 B.C.) and underwent numerous expansions in the centuries following. The Jerusalem area was inhabited in the Early Bronze I period (*ca.* 3150–2850 B.C.) and perhaps even earlier. But some kind of town existed here in the twentieth to nineteenth centuries B.C. and continued on until the present day. The site of Dothan goes back to the Early Bronze age when it was a large settlement surrounded by a wall. Occupation continued into Arab times. Nothing can be said of Gerar (Tell Abu Hureirah on the Wadi esh-Shari'ah to the south of Lachish) until the mound is excavated.

This brief discussion points to the possibility that events narrated in Genesis could have taken place early in the second millennium if all that was required in dating these events was that certain places referred to in the narrative existed in the early part of the second millennium. However, most of these towns also existed much later and some of them continuously for hundreds of years so that the narratives could be accepted as suiting geographical conditions over a long period of time.

As to personal names like Abraham, Isaac, Jacob, we are able to say today that these were current names in the areas referred to in the Bible. The details have been collected by a variety of writers in recent years. The Amorites in particular were fond of names of the type of Jacob and Isaac, names which are really verbal forms. However, a chronological problem attaches to names. The name Abraham (A-ba-am-ra-am in one form) appears under several variants in

32. Details about excavations at these sites are available in the *Encyclopedia of Archaeological Excavations in the Holy Land* (*EAEHL*), 4 vols. (1975, 1976, 1977, 1978).

Professor Nelson Glueck examines a piece of pottery from Abraham's time. (Israel Office of Information)

Akkadian and Amorite contexts over many centuries. It has several parallels in the same contexts, indicating that this type of name was widely current in nearly every period from which names of West Semitic peoples have been preserved. Certainly the name was common enough in the first half of the second millennium B.C.

The same observations may be made about names like Isaac, Jacob, and Israel. Unfortunately the name patterns alone do not enable us to date the patriarchal period with any sort of exactness.[33]

An analysis of the beasts of burden of Abraham and the other patriarchs shows that these were camels and asses. The asses seem to have been used more widely than the camels. It has been argued that camels were not used in the East at this time. This cannot be maintained any longer. It is probably true that camels had not come into very general use in Abraham's time. It was more like 1300 B.C. before this beast of burden became popular. However, there is clear evidence that the camel was used somewhat in earlier times. Small clay figures, some carvings, and some pieces of camel bone and camel hair are known from graves in both Egypt and Mesopotamia before 2000 B.C.[34] There is no need to regard these references in the patriarchal narratives, therefore, as anachronisms.

33. For a thorough discussion of this point see T. L. Thompson, *op. cit.*, pp. 17–51; J. van Seters, *Abraham in History and Tradition*, pp. 39–64.
34. J. P. Free, *JNES*, Vol. III (1944), pp. 187–193.

The whole question of the beginnings of the domestication of the camel is extremely complex. A South Arabian origin for the domestic camel is widely accepted today. Moreover, the manner of domestication varied widely in character since the camel may be and has been milked, ridden, loaded with baggage, eaten, harnessed to a plow or wagon, traded for goods or wives, turned into sandals and camel-hair coats, etc. The references in Middle Eastern literature to the camel from the later centuries of the second millennium B.C. give no clue to the process of domestication, which preceded such references. But the domestication of the camel must have been known in Northern Arabia and Syria much earlier. One recent study proposes that the process of camel domestication first got under way between 3000 and 2500 B.C.[35] Since it is impossible to fix a date for Abraham with any certainty, we need to exercise caution in regarding the reference to camels in passages like Genesis 12:16; 24:10, 19f., 22, 31f., 35, 46, 61, 64; 37:25 as a pure anachronism.[36]

THE CUSTOMS PORTRAYED IN THE PATRIARCHAL NARRATIVES

One of the most important contributions of modern archaeology to our understanding of the Bible is the information which is given about the laws and customs of the people. This material comes either from the formal law codes or from the many incidental references to the customs of the people to be found on the documents of everyday life such as receipts, letters, contracts, licenses, and the like.

We now have a great deal of this kind of material, in particular from patriarchal times. In the first place, we know of at least three Amorite law codes, one of which is complete, namely, the code of the great Hammurabi. But this code was but the later expression of the earlier codes of the town of Eshnunna and of the king Lipit Ishtar.[37] In the second place, we have a great variety of baked-clay tablets which give us remarkable glimpses into the customs of the ordinary people of the day.

One of the most interesting collections of written records is that of the ancient Hurrian town of Nuzi which lay to the east of the Tigris River. Its modern name is Yorghan Tepe. Here, in the years 1925 to 1931, Professor Chiera and his colleagues of the American Schools of Oriental Research found some 20,000 clay documents in the family archives of several of the villas of the town.[38] The date of these documents is given by the excavators as the fifteenth century B.C., which may be as much as three or four hundred years later than

35. R. W. Bulliet, *The Camel and the Wheel* (Cambridge, Mass., 1975), ch. 2, pp. 28–56, esp. p. 56.
36. E. A. Speiser, *Genesis* (New York, 1964), p. 90.
37. J. B. Pritchard, *ANET*, pp. 159–163.
38. R. H. Pfeiffer and E. A. Speiser, *One Hundred New Selected Nuzi Texts* (New Haven, 1936).

A beautiful example of Akkadian craftsman-ship ca. 2300 B.C. This bronze head, pre-sumably of Sargon I, was cast and then de-tailed further with a chisel. It is rather stylized and nearly perfectly symmetrical, but note the realism of the combed waves of the beard. (Consulate General, Republic of Iraq)

the traditional date of the patriarch Abraham (eighteen century B.C. or even earlier); but because customs persist, the tablets give important evidence about the legal and social structure of society in these lands in previous centuries.

But insights into the life of the people of Mesopotamia in the centuries that spanned the patriarchal period have come from other significant collections of tablets as well, including those from Mari,[39] Alalakh,[40] and small collections from numerous sites in Mesopotamia and Syria. What promises to be a remark-able collection of some 20,000 or more tablets has been found in ancient Ebla (Tell Mardikh) in Syria. These tablets come from about 2300 B.C. and were contemporary with the great Sargon I of Akkad who founded the first Semitic

39. Their publication in volumes of *Archives Royales de Mari* (ARM) will take many years to complete.

40. D. J. Wiseman, *The Alalakh Tablets* (1953).

An example of the private cylinder seals with which Babylonians signed their documents. The seal was rolled across a clay tablet when the clay was still wet. (Consulate General, Republic of Iraq)

empire about 2350 B.C. He briefly subdued Ebla and other cities, but on his death two of his sons successively lost most of their father's empire. His grandson Naram-Sin (*ca.* 2250) restored the dominion of Akkad and destroyed Ebla. The archives of Ebla show that Ebla was in its day a strong rival of Akkad. We are now on the way to being able to study the life of people in northern Mesopotamia some 500 years before the traditional date of the patriarchs.

When the Nuzi documents were first published there was an enthusiastic response by biblical scholars to the information they contained, for they seemed to cast a great deal of light on a social milieu which appeared to be very similar to the society of the patriarchs.[41] More mature reflection on the material from Nuzi has led scholars to the conclusion that parallels occur between the patriarchal narratives and cuneiform texts from various parts of the ancient Near East at various times, so that the uniqueness of the relationship with Nuzi has been called into question. This later research has made it difficult to use these parallels in nonbiblical sources as a guide for dating, although their value in assisting our understanding of the society of the ancient Near East in the second millennium B.C. is undoubted and at present the large majority of relevant social parallels come from the second millennium B.C. The patriarchal customs were quite at home in the Mesopotamian culture of that period. We may infer that the biblical traditions in Genesis 12–50 which portray a thorough acquaintance with a Mesopotamian way of life came with the original migrants from Mesopotamia. And the general period must have been the earlier part of the second millennium since there was no long-term association with Mesopotamia

41. C. H. Gordon, "Biblical Customs and the Nuzi Tablets," *BA* (Feb., 1940); H. H. Rowley, "Recent Discovery and the Patriarchal Age," *BJRL* (Sept., 1949), etc.

in the first millennium B.C. to provide such an intimate acquaintance with these Mesopotamian customs.

Let us turn then to a discussion of some of the more important of these customs. It will be our method to refer to the Mesopotamian custom first and then to draw out some biblical parallels. For convenience we shall deal first with such major items as inheritance and marriage, and then refer briefly to one or two miscellaneous customs.

In Mesopotamia, inheritance was of major importance. Property was, theoretically at least, inalienable and could not pass from the family. In order to overcome this difficulty a fictitious system of adoption was used. By this device it was possible for a man to adopt any number of "sons" or "brothers," and then to pass over the property rights quite legally to the adopted party. Cases are known where there was a regular traffic in this kind of adoption.

A property owner who had no son would normally adopt an heir. The adopted "son" might be a freeborn man, a slave, or a relative. The tablet of adoption was written on clay after proclamation at the gate of the city. When party A adopted party B, he willed to B the major portion of his lands, buildings, and other items, in consideration of the fact that B promised to serve A during

Daggers and a sheath, ca. 2600 B.C., from Ur. The handles are made of lapis lazuli studded with gold; the smooth blades and filigreed sheath are also gold. Note the mark of the craftsman or owner on some of the blades. (Consulate General, Republic of Iraq)

These copper miniatures (ca. 3000 B.C.) are fine examples of Sumerian art. The chariot, from Tell Agrab, is one of the earliest depictions of this vehicle; the driver straddles a centerboard and is drawn by four asses. The statuette of the wrestlers was found at Khafaje, east of Baghdad. The wrestlers wear only belts and may carry the large jars on a test of skill. (Consulate General, Republic of Iraq)

A's lifetime and then undertook to give him a decent burial on his death. There was generally a proviso that if A had no son, B would inherit the property outright. If, however, A had a son subsequent to the signing of the adoption document, then the natural son would become the heir and take the father's "gods," which were generally small clay figures used in family worship, but which seem to have become in time something like our modern title deeds. At any rate, the man who owned the property possessed the gods, and he passed these over when the property came into the possession of another.

There was another possibility that could arise in the case of a man who had no son. It was quite common for the man's wife to take a slave woman and present her to her husband in order to raise up a child for herself. In this case the son of the slave woman became the heir if there were no other sons. But here, too, should there be in due course a son born to the first wife, then the son of the slave woman took second place and had to surrender the inheritance to the true son. It was provided, however, that in that case the son of the slave woman should not be cast out but should have some share in the inheritance.

But there were in fact four possibilities available in the ancient Near East in cases where a childless couple lacked a son. They could adopt a son, the husband could marry a second wife, the husband might obtain a son through union with his concubine, or the wife might provide the husband with a slave girl. These solutions appear in texts from many periods and places, although all four were practiced at Nuzi. One of the most famous of the Nuzi texts is the Adoption Text HSS 5, 67.[42] This contract contains a clause that if the wife provided by the adopting man for his adopted son proved barren, she had to give a Lullu woman (i.e., a slave girl) to her husband although the first wife would exercise authority over any children born to the slave girl. In this respect this tablet provides a good parallel to the patriarchal narratives since the three elements of a barren wife, the wife's initiative in obtaining a slave girl, and the authority of the wife over the children occur in such passages as Genesis 16:2; 30:1-4, 9.

The Nuzi tablet in question reads as follows:

> The tablet of adoption belonging to Zike, the son of Akkuya: he gave his son Shennima in adoption to Shuriha-ilu, and Shuriha-ilu, with reference to Shennima, from all the lands . . . and his earnings of every sort gave to Shennima one portion of his property. If Shuriha-ilu should have a son of his own, as the principal son he shall take a double share; Shennima shall then be next in order and take his proper share. As long as Shuriha-ilu is alive, Shennima shall revere him. When Shuriha-ilu dies, Shennima shall become the heir. Furthermore, Kelim-ninu has been given in marriage to Shennima. If Kelim-ninu bears children, Shennima shall not take another wife; but if Kelim-ninu does not bear, Kelim-ninu shall acquire a woman of the land of Lullu as wife for Shennima, and Kelim-ninu may not send the offspring away. Any sons that may be born to Shennima from the womb of Kelim-ninu, to those sons shall be given all the lands and buildings of every sort. However, if she does not bear a son, then the daughter of Kelim-ninu from the lands and buildings shall take one portion of the property. Furthermore, Shuriha-ilu shall not adopt another son in addition to Shennima.[43]

This general custom according to which a barren wife gave her slave girl to her husband to raise children is known in a variety of texts apart from Nuzi. In some of these the practice was confined to priestesses in a restricted application of the same principle.[44] But Hammurabi Law 163 applied this provision to an ordinary wife and other old Babylonian texts refer to a girl who acted as a slave for the wife and a concubine for the husband.

42. See J. B. Pritchard, ANET, p. 220.
43. Ibid.
44. Hammurabi Law 144.

But there are other items of interest on this tablet. There is the provision that a handmaiden shall be given as a gift on the occasion of the marriage of Shennima to Kelim-ninu, and a proviso that if Shennima takes another wife besides Kelim-ninu after Kelim-ninu has borne children, then Kelim-ninu may take certain action against him.

The inclusion of a female slave in a dowry is mentioned in three old Babylonian marriage contracts (cf. Gen. 24:59, 61).

It must be noted, however, that the Nuzi tablet quoted is the only example of this exact custom, for five other Nuzi marriage contracts make provision for the husband to marry a second wife if the first was barren, and four imply that the husband could raise up offspring through his concubine in similar circumstances.

There was thus a good deal of flexibility in the arrangement, and the biblical narratives indicate only one of these.

With these illustrations of Mesopotamian law before us we may draw a number of comparisons between the customs of the patriarchs and those of the people of northern Mesopotamia as depicted here.

It would seem that in the first attempt of Abraham to secure an heir he resorted to the current practice of adopting a slave as his heir. It was "Eliezer of Damascus" who was chosen as heir and he was to Abraham "one born in my house" (Gen. 15:2, 3). At a later stage Abraham resorted to the method of taking a subsidiary wife. Actually the Bible makes the point quite clearly that it was Sarah the wife of Abraham who invited Abraham to take this woman. "It may be that I may obtain children by her" was Sarah's hope (Gen. 16:2).

When Ishmael was born, he presumably was regarded as the heir of Abraham. However, in due course Sarah herself gave birth to a son Isaac, who quite naturally took the place of Ishmael. Sarah wanted to cast out the bondwoman and her son, but this thing was very grievous in the eyes of Abraham (Gen. 21:10, 11). While Sarah does not seem to have had a great deal of compunction about this suggestion, it was, of course, quite out of keeping with the customs of the land, and Abraham revolted at the thought. Only a divine injunction led Abraham to allow the child and his mother to depart (Gen. 21:12).

Our discussion has already touched briefly on marriage. A study of some of the ways of the ancient Middle East is instructive here, too, because there are interesting parallels between these Mesopotamian customs and the biblical customs found in the stories of the patriarchs.

A number of other biblical parallels with ancient Middle Eastern practice may be illustrated from the following Nuzi document, which is the adoption tablet of a certain Nashwi who adopted a certain Wullu:

> The adoption tablet of Nashwi son of Arshenni. He adopted Wullu son of Puhishenni. As long as Nashwi lives, Wullu shall give him food and clothing. When Nashwi dies, Wullu shall be the heir. Should Nashwi beget a son, the latter shall divide equally with Wullu, but only

Nashwi's son shall take Nashwi's gods. But if there be no son of Nashwi, then Wullu shall take Nashwi's gods. And Nashwi had given his daughter Nuhuya as a wife to Wullu. And if Wullu takes another wife, he forfeits Nashwi's land and buildings. Whoever breaks the contract shall pay one mina of silver, and one mina of gold.[45]

In Genesis 29:24, 29 Laban gave both his daughters a maid as a marriage gift. The same custom is clear in the above document. It is also to be found in the document already quoted, which continues beyond the point given in our quotation with the words:

Furthermore, Yalampa is given as a handmaid to Kelim-ninu and Shatim-ninu has been made a co-parent. As long as she is alive she (i.e. Yalampa) shall revere her and Shatim-ninu shall not annul the (agreement). If Kelim-ninu bears (children) and Shennima takes another wife, she may take her dowry and leave.

The practice of providing a maid as a marriage gift was quite common in ancient Mesopotamia. In fact it continued until the Neo-Babylonian and Persian periods. It is not therefore of any special significance for dating purposes, although it is of value in portraying a general cultural milieu.

Again, the demand made by Laban on Jacob that he should not take another wife besides the two daughters and that he should not ill-treat the daughters (Gen. 31:51–54) occurs in a number of Nuzi texts and in Old Assyrian contracts.[46] The first text quoted above, the adoption tablet of Zike, contains this provision. This practice was also continued for many centuries and occurs in marriage contracts of the Neo-Babylonian and Persian periods.

When the Nuzi tablets were first published, writers like C. H. Gordon argued that the Jacob-Laban narratives could be understood in terms of an adoption arrangement between Jacob and Laban. This view has not commended itself to later scholars[47] and should probably not be pressed. The reference to Laban's *teraphim* (household gods), which were stolen by Rachel (Gen. 31:19, 33–35), is another feature in the Jacob-Laban story which earlier writers thought lent support to the idea of adoption. It was argued that Rachel stole the gods in order to guarantee Jacob's claim to the inheritance. However, since he was leaving the country, one wonders what value the possession of the household gods would have been. This much is clear. A number of Nuzi texts do refer to household gods (*teraphim*), and in nine of them the gods were given as part of an inheritance. Yet it was not merely the possession of the *teraphim* that guaranteed

45. J. B. Pritchard, ANET, pp. 219f., Tablet 2.
46. See J. B. Pritchard, ANET³, p. 543, document 4.
47. M. J. Selman, "The Social Environment of the Patriarchs," *Tyndale Bulletin*, No. 21 (1976), pp. 123–125; J. van Seters, *Abraham in History and Tradition*, pp. 78–85; T. L. Thompson, *op. cit.*, pp. 269–480.

Left: A bronze statuette, originally covered with gold or silver foil, of a Syrian god, possibly Baal. The kilt and headdress are Egyptian in style. It was found near Tyre and is dated ca. *1400 B.C. (British Museum) Right: Limestone votive statue, found in the Abu temple at Eshnunna (Tell Asmar). (Consulate General, Republic of Iraq)*

the inheritance but also the father's act of bequeathing them.[48] In the Nuzi texts there were also heirs who participated in the division of the inheritance who did not receive the gods, which were normally given to the eldest son, though not automatically. But there is another interesting feature here: it was not unusual for Mesopotamians to carry *teraphim* with them when they went to another country.[49]

Despite a number of uncertainties in the drawing of parallelisms one cannot but be impressed with a number of features in the Bible and in ancient Near

48. See M. Greenberg, "Another Look at Rachel's Theft of Teraphim," *JBL*, Vol. 81 (1962), pp. 239–248.

49. Cf. M. Greenberg, *op. cit.*, pp. 246ff.; T. L. Thompson, *op. cit.*, pp. 277f.; M. J. Selman, *op. cit.*, p. 124.

Eastern documents which point to a community of ideas and practices. There are, of course, always variants of a particular practice as one moves from place to place.

The story of Abraham's purchase of the cave of Machpelah as a burial site for Sarah his wife (Gen. 22) is an instructive one since it gives information about a variety of customs relating to the procedures to be followed in the purchase of land. As a foreigner or landless resident alien (Hebrew ger $w^e\underline{t}\hat{o}\check{s}\underline{a}\underline{b}$) Abraham was required to approach the local citizens or sons of Heth (cf. Gen. 10:15). Exaggerated politeness and protracted negotiations which are characteristic of oriental business dealings then took place, as was normal, at the city gate (Gen. 23:10). Abraham wanted only the cave, but he was obliged finally to take the whole field. The price was fixed at 400 pieces of silver—a mere bagatelle, they said (v. 15). The silver was weighed out on simple scale pans, presumably according to the standard weights used by the merchants (v. 16). The area in question was carefully defined (v. 17) and finally recognized as Abraham's property by the citizens, and Sarah was buried. It was the first piece of the promised land that Abraham could call his own.

The whole story has been interpreted in the light of Hittite laws.[50] Two of the Hittite laws which were used to explain the transaction are concerned with the feudal service which was associated with the property from which the owner was anxious to be free.[51] But once it is realized that the Hittites in the story are really a Canaanite group (Gen. 10:15), the Hittite association loses its significance. It was not a question of feudal dues at all, but simply a land sale in which the owner drove a hard bargain when he found someone in desperate need.

But despite this recognition that the story does not concern the Anatolian Hittites, it has many general characteristics in common with Near Eastern legal procedures from many periods. Thus the phrase "for the full price" (v. 9), which occurs also in the account of David's purchase of the threshing floor (I Chron. 21:23, 24), is the equivalent of an expression which occurs with slight variations in Akkadian sale contracts from several periods. Indeed, it runs back to Sumerian times. The expression occurs in the Mari texts and the Alalakh tablets, as well as in later texts, to denote that the complete price had been paid, with no balance remaining. What Abraham was saying was that he would give the full value of the field, that is, he would buy it. Allowing for minor variations in expressions, we are here dealing with a well-known legal formula.[52] As in most ancient Near Eastern deeds, the exact price of the sale is mentioned (v. 16) and the account of the transfer includes a description of the property (v. 17) in terms of the type of real estate (field), the name of the landlord, the general location (Machpelah), and the appurtenances of the land (cave and trees). However, the story in Genesis 23 does not mention guarantee clauses or provisions against

---

50. M. R. Lehmann, "Abraham's Purchase of Machpelah and Hittite Law," *BASOR*, No. 129 (Feb., 1953), pp. 15–18.

51. See Laws 46 and 47 of the Hittite Code, *ANET*[3], p. 191.

52. G. M. Tucker, "The Legal Background of Genesis 23," *JBL*, Vol. 85 (1966), pp. 77–84.

suit, supported often by penalties. No list of witnesses is given, although this may be implied by the phrase "in the presence of the sons of Heth before all who went in at the gate of his city." But then, Genesis 23 is not a legal document but a narrative about title deeds. The procedures in evidence here carried on into the first millennium so that we are not able to link this story to a specific century or several centuries. But the style, structure, formulae, and contents of certain parts of the report are modeled on deeds of sale well known in the ancient Near East. The reader is thus enabled to see more clearly the meaning and context of the various elements of the story, thus enabling him to discern the significance of some of the details which are important for interpretation.

We have not exhausted the possibilities of such a study as this. The tells of the ancient Middle East still contain an untold wealth of tablet records which will throw light on the biblical period. At the moment, after a period of what seemed a growing clarity in our understanding of patriarchal times, we have become somewhat bewildered by the mass of data requiring careful reconsideration. And each year produces more and more tablets which will throw additional light on a puzzling age. But already we sense that the biblical narratives provide evidence of a society which, if it appears strange to modern readers, now seems to be realistic and authentic. We lack the sort of information which will enable us to pinpoint exactly the patriarchal era, but we have gained enormously from our understanding of social and legal practice in the ancient Middle East of the second millennium B.C. If we are not in a position to declare beyond question that the patriarchs fit into the first part of the second millennium B.C., we are certainly not in a position to deny such a proposition. Even if some of the customs were operative over many centuries, it is also true to say that they were operative in the period 2000–1500 B.C.

Some support for this view comes from an interesting line of research which has been initiated in recent years, namely, a consideration of the character of the major West Semitic tribal groups on the middle Euphrates in the nineteenth

Another cylinder seal and its impression (ca. 2000 B.C.). The two human figures, the tree, and the snake have been thought to depict a Babylonian version of the temptation of Eve, but no proof has been found in cuneiform texts. (British Museum)

and eighteenth centuries B.C. The important documents excavated at Mari dating to this general period have provided a wealth of data and have enabled a study of the relationships between the tribal groups and large urban centers like Mari. The two groups lived in a kind of equilibrium with one another, with a constant interchange between the pastoralists and the urban settlers who formed a dimorphic (two-shape) society.[53] Some workers in this field have seen close parallels between the Mari society and the society of the patriarchs[54] and have expressed a preference for the Middle Bronze Age (ca. 1800–1550) for patriarchal backgrounds. The picture that is painted in these more recent discussions is of a society living in simple villages on the nearer or further outskirts of large towns like Mari, tribally organized but having many contacts with urban society. They were sheep-breeders who moved their encampments periodically, normally annually, in search of water and pasturage. At points of contact between the two societies there were recognized modes of procedure. It has been further argued[55] that there is archaeological evidence in Palestine at the site of Givat Sharet for a "dimorphic society." Here a small unwalled satellite village comprising a mere dozen or so simple courtyard houses was built along a straggling path on a hillside about three-quarters of a mile southeast of the fortified Middle Bronze Age site of Bethshemesh in Palestine, and contemporary with it.[56] The houses show only one basic building type, and the pottery is homogeneous and contemporary with Middle Bronze Bethshemesh. Thereafter the village was abandoned. The date was about the eighteenth century B.C., that is, the Mari Age. To date, other examples have not been found, but this may be due to the lack of excavation, and it seems likely that others will be discovered. But that is a task yet to be undertaken.

It is evident that archaeological research has by no means completed its task in reference to the patriarchal period, and many fruitful avenues have yet to be explored more fully. We have by no means exhausted the study of the total cultural background of the ancient Near East. Only against that background can we come to a clear understanding of the background of the patriarchs. But progress is being made as scholars give attention to the further analysis of the social milieu of the patriarchs as reflected in Genesis; to the evidence of the ancient Near Eastern society as reflected in the numerous commercial and legal texts that are available; to the evidence of the Mari texts for the light they throw on the tribal societies of the Mari Age; and to the cultural history of Syria-Palestine as it is being reconstructed by modern archaeology.

53. J. T. Luke, *Pastoralism and Politics in the Mari Period* (1965), and V. H. Matthews, *Pastoral Nomadism in the Mari Kingdom (ca. 1830–1760 B.C.)* (1978), represent this line of research.
54. E.g., W. G. Dever, "Prolegomenon to a reconsideration of archaeology and patriarchal backgrounds," in J. H. Hayes and J. M. Miller, *Israelite and Judaean History*, pp. 102–120.
55. W. G. Dever, *op. cit.*, pp. 111f.
56. C. Epstein, "Bethshemesh," *IEJ*, Vol. XXII (1972), p. 157; D. Bahat, "Beth-shemesh," *IEJ*, Vol. XXIII (1973), pp. 246f.

3

IN THE LAND OF THE PHARAOHS

THERE must be few people who have never heard of the noble Joseph who was
sold by his brothers into Egypt and rose to a place of prominence in that land. In
due course he was able to have his whole family, numbering seventy people,
brought to this new land. If we ask whether there is Egyptian evidence for the
rise of this very Joseph to fame, the answer is that up to the present we have no
formal evidence for the Bible stories about Joseph and his family. However,
students of the history of Egypt have brought to light in recent years a considerable number of important facts which furnish a background into which the
biblical narratives fit very naturally. This is the sort of thing we have seen in the
case of the patriarchs. We shall see it again and again in this book.

THE COMING OF THE HYKSOS RULERS TO EGYPT

We must digress at this point to refer briefly to some facts of Egyptian history.
Historians recognize some thirty more or less well-defined dynasties covering the
period of Egyptian history from about 3000 B.C. to Roman times. In patriarchal
times it was probably the Twelfth Dynasty that ruled Egypt. This line of rulers
came to an end about 1786 B.C., to be succeeded by Dynasties Thirteen and
Fourteen. The Thirteenth Dynasty (ca. 1786–1633 B.C.) ruled from Thebes but
eventually lost their authority and became vassals of Asiatic newcomers who had
been infiltrating the Delta region during the declining years of the Thirteenth
Dynasty. These foreigners were groups of several western Asiatic peoples, chiefly
Semites forced southward by widespread disturbances in lands to the north and
east of Egypt. The tribal leaders or sheikhs of these people were called "Princes

41

Scenes from the so-called Ani Papyrus (ca. 1300 B.C.), one of the papyri of the Book of the Dead. Ani was a royal scribe and governor of the granaries. In the middle scene the heart of a soul is being weighed against a feather in the judgment hall of the god Osiris. The Ani Papyrus is a roll seventy-six feet long and fifteen inches wide. (British Museum)

of the Desert Uplands" or "Rulers of Foreign Countries" (Hikau-khoswet, hence Hyksos). The last rulers of the Thirteenth Dynasty[1] became vassals of the Hyksos rulers. The Fourteenth Dynasty (*ca.* 1786–1603 B.C.) rulers, of which there were over seventy who reigned for the most part for very brief periods, operated from ancient Memphis (Ithet-Tawy) in the north until they were replaced by the Hyksos rulers who formed the Fifteenth and Sixteenth "Hyksos" Dynasties and ruled for roughly 140 years. They established a second capital in the eastern Delta at Avaris. These Semitic "pharaohs" took upon themselves the full rank and style of the local Egyptian kings and used the Egyptian state administration, employing regular Egyptian officials in the manner of the old regime. In the course of time naturalized Semitic officials took over many of these offices. Among these was a certain Hur, who was a kind of chancellor.

Eventually a line of princes from southern or Upper Egypt were able to rise and throw out the Hyksos rulers. A certain Kamose was able to re-occupy all Egypt for the Egyptians except Avaris in the northeast Delta. His successor Ahmose I founded the Eighteenth Dynasty and expelled the Hyksos rulers completely *ca.* 1570 B.C.

1. R. M. Engberg, *The Hyksos Reconsidered* (Chicago, 1939); A. Alt, *Die Herkunft der Hyksos in neuer Sicht* (Munich, 1954), pp. 26ff.; J. van Seters, *The Hyksos, a New Investigation* (New Haven, 1966); W. C. Hayes, *Cambridge Ancient History*, Vol. II, ch. II (1962).

We have a special interest in such a group because in the later chapters of Genesis we find the patriarchal family settling into their new home in Egypt, apparently with the goodwill of the rulers of the land. At a later day, when a "king arose who knew not Joseph," we find that the Israelite group was ill-treated. We conclude that at an earlier date the rulers were not Egyptians but people who were sympathetic to the patriarchal family itself and perhaps related to it in a broad ethnic sense. The Hyksos rulers would fit into this category very well.

WHAT THE HYKSOS RULERS GAVE TO EGYPT

Let us outline some facts about these people. Despite the fact that the Egyptians did all in their power to destroy all record of them once they had cast them out, they brought a great deal to Egypt that was to be for the benefit of the Egyptians themselves.[2] We now know that the rulers of the Eighteenth Dynasty went to great lengths to erase all traces of these Hyksos rulers. Their names were cut out of the monuments and every written record that could be found was destroyed. Only the keen eyes of the modern archaeologist have been able to discover clear evidence of the Hyksos invaders and to give us a picture of their achievements. These Hyksos rulers were, for the most part, of western Semitic stock, that is to say, they were largely Canaanite in origin. They evidently had a widespread empire in their time, for objects such as scarabs, which belong specifically to their culture, have been found in many lands in the East. Their most famous king was Khayan, whose name has been found on inscribed material in Egypt, Palestine, Mesopotamia, and even in Crete. This suggests that they had wide trade connections all over the East.

Many new features were introduced into Egypt at this time. We think today

2. J. A. Wilson, *The Burden of Egypt* (Chicago, 1951), ch. 7.

Tomb model of an Egyptian death ship carrying the mummified body to the underworld and "fields of peace." (British Museum)

Blue faience tile (sixteenth-fourteenth centuries B.C.) with a drawing in black of a typical Hyksos chariot, a driver, and two horses. The Hyksos introduced horses and chariots into Egypt. (Metropolitan Museum of Art, gift of J. Pierpont Morgan, 1917)

that the Hyksos people brought to Egypt such items as the horse and chariot, new types of daggers and swords, the strong compound Asiatic bow, and new types of fortification. Of special interest were the huge earth ramparts which enclosed fortified areas where chariots were housed. These have been found in several places in Palestine and Syria, as well as in Egypt. At places like Jericho and Shechem in Palestine great fortifications of this age were found during excavations there. It seems that Palestine itself was organized in a feudal manner at this time and consisted of numerous little states which owed allegiance to the Hyksos king.

PALESTINE IN THE SEVENTEENTH AND SIXTEENTH CENTURIES B.C.

In Palestine there was evidently great prosperity, if we are to judge from the wealth of the graves of the Canaanites of this period. These are among the richest of the tombs of all time in Palestine. During these years numerous new towns were built in the hill areas. Despite the picture of overall prosperity and of great urban development, there was evidently no public security, for there were many occasions when the towns were destroyed with violence. Excavation shows layers of burning in several towns dating back to this period. At no time in the history of Palestine were there so many walled towns in the land. We are quite naturally reminded of the spies of Moses who visited the land and reported, "The cities are walled, *and* very great" (Num. 13:28).

Joseph came from Palestine and was later able to arrange for the migration of his aged father Jacob and his brothers from his homeland to Egypt. There are many lines of evidence to suggest that it was during the Hyksos period that the events of Genesis 40–50 took place. We may suggest that Joseph came to prominence in Egypt about 1700 B.C.

THE HYKSOS CAPITAL AT AVARIS

The Hyksos rulers conquered northern Egypt and placed their capital in the Delta area, calling it Avaris. It seems that they allowed the Egyptians to con-tinue to exercise some sort of governing power from a local capital at Thebes some four hundred miles up the Nile, although this authority was naturally supervised by the Hyksos rulers. Once the Hyksos conquerors were expelled, the town of Thebes again became the capital of Egypt.

The town of Avaris has been the subject of some discussion among the experts in recent years. Its location is now known with practical certainty. The land of Goshen, referred to as the area to which Jacob and his sons came, was in all probability the area around the Wadi Tumilat, which lay quite close to the capital of the Hyksos kings but a little to the southeast.

We have some reason to think that the new rulers, while they brought a good deal to Egypt, learned a great deal from Egypt. They soon adopted all sorts of ways and customs that were current in the land. For example, they copied Egyptian methods of writing and imitated the religious zeal of the Egyptians by building many new temples. An ancient god of Egypt, Seth by name, was honored in Avaris as Seth-Sutekh. This god bore a close resemblance to some of the Asiatic gods like Ba'al. His garments, headdress, and horns of divinity were Asiatic in type.

It is of some interest that when Horemhab, the last ruler of the Eighteenth Dynasty, was pharaoh (ca. 1340–1310), a vizier of Egypt named Seti came to the city of Tanis in the Delta region about the year 1330 B.C. to celebrate a four-hundredth anniversary. This took the form of the worship of the Egyptian god Seth, who is represented on the stele set up to celebrate his anniversary as an Asiatic deity in Asiatic dress. Some four hundred years earlier the Hyksos had begun their rule in Egypt in Avaris. The celebration thus commemorated the four-hundredth year of the rule of Seth as king and the four-hundredth year of the founding of Tanis. The Egyptians would not mention the hated Hyksos in such a commemoration, but the inference may be drawn. The vizier Seti later became the pharaoh Seti I, and the name Seti means "Seth's man."[3]

The Hyksos honored other gods besides Seth.[4]

In matters of court procedure we think that the Hyksos rulers took over a

3. J. B. Pritchard, ANET, pp. 252f.
4. J. van Seters, op. cit., pp. 171–180.